As one of the world's longest established and best-known travel brands, Thomas Cook are the experts in travel.

For more than 135 years our guidebooks have unlocked the secrets of destinations around the world, sharing with travellers a wealth of experience and a passion for travel.

Rely on Thomas Cook as your travelling companion on your next trip and benefit from our unique heritage.

Thomas Cook **pocket** guides

BRISTOL

Bristol Libraries

D1148338

Thomas Cook

Written by Laura Dixon

Published by Thomas Cook Publishing
A division of Thomas Cook Tour Operations Limited
Company registration no. 3772199 England
The Thomas Cook Business Park, Unit 9, Coningsby Road
Peterborough PE3 8SB, United Kingdom
Email: books@thomascook.com, Tel: +44 (0)1733 416477
www.thomascookpublishing.com

Produced by Cambridge Publishing Management Limited
Burr Elm Court, Main Street, Caldecote CB23 7NU
www.cambridgepm.co.uk

ISBN: 978-1-84848-460-3

This first edition © 2010 Thomas Cook Publishing
Text © Thomas Cook Publishing
Cartography supplied by Redmoor Design, Tavistock, Devon
Map data © OpenStreetMap contributors CC-BY-SA,
www.openstreetmap.org, www.creativecommons.org

Series Editor: Karen Beaulah
Production/DTP: Steven Collins

Printed and bound in Spain by GraphyCems

Cover photography © Thomas Cook Publishing

All rights reserved. No part of this publication may be reproduced, stored in
a retrieval system or transmitted, in any form or by any means, electronic,
mechanical, recording or otherwise, in any part of the world, without prior
permission of the publisher. Requests for permission should be made to the
publisher at the above address.

Although every care has been taken in compiling this publication, and the contents
are believed to be correct at the time of printing, Thomas Cook Tour Operations
Limited cannot accept any responsibility for errors or omissions, however caused,
or for changes in details given in the guidebook, or for the consequences of any
reliance on the information provided. Descriptions and assessments are based on
the author's views and experiences when writing and do not necessarily represent
those of Thomas Cook Tour Operations Limited.

CONTENTS

SYMBOLS KEY

The following symbols are used throughout this book:

ⓐ address **ⓣ** telephone **ⓕ** fax **ⓦ** website address **ⓔ** email
ⓛ opening times **Ⓝ** public transport connections **ⓘ** important

The following symbols are used on the maps:

𝒊 information office		O	city
✈ airport		O	large town
✚ hospital		○	small town
⛨ police station		=	motorway
🚌 bus station		—	main road
🚆 railway station		—	minor road
✝ cathedral		—	railway
POI (point of interest)			
❶ numbers denote featured cafés, restaurants & venues			

PRICE CATEGORIES

The ratings below indicate average price rates for a double room per night, including breakfast:
£ under £100 ££ £100–150 £££ over £150
The typical cost for a three-course meal without drinks, is as follows:
£ under £20 ££ £20–40 £££ over £40

▶ Banksy's 'Mild Mild West' scene is one of Bristol's landmarks

INTRODUCING
Bristol

Introduction

Bristol used to be known as the city of Brunel, balloons and bridges, but these days we can add one more B to the list: Banksy. Whatever you think of the graffiti artist, his impact on his home town has been immeasurable, with a 2009 guerrilla takeover of Bristol City Museum and Art Gallery bringing in over £10 million at the height of the recession and establishing Bristol as a city to visit.

The capital city of the southwest is a bridge between Devon, Somerset and Cornwall, and the rest of the UK – it has that rare mixture of being laid-back and fully functioning, and the quality of life is better here than elsewhere in the country. Where else will you find offices closing at 4pm on a Friday so that their staff can make it to the beach for a post-work surf? There's a very definite atmosphere of work to live, rather than live to work, which makes a break here relaxing, fun and eminently repeatable, so much so that many weekend breakers leave with a dream of a more permanent holiday here.

Bristol is made up of a patchwork of villages, each with a distinct personality, giving it a bohemian and eclectic feel. The city centre is the most corporate area; Clifton and the West End have a more rarefied air, while the harbourside and waterfront area has become the new hotspot in terms of regeneration, attractions and swanky apartments. Further afield, arty/hippy areas such as St Werburghs and Totterdown are attracting creative types, whereas St Pauls and Easton are diverse and multicultural.

In terms of sights, Bristol doesn't have a serious checklist. You won't feel short-changed if you miss out on all the ten key attractions – but you will miss out if you take things too quickly. One of the beauties of the place is its slower pace of life. Sip your cider slowly, watch the water flow by and immerse yourself in a city where faster isn't better, time is your own and the best things in life are free.

🔺 *Ashton Court is a grand estate across Clifton Suspension Bridge*

When to go

SEASONS & CLIMATE

Bristol is a summer city. The tenor of the place changes
once the sun comes out, with picnickers in the park, drinkers
spilling out into the streets and many festivals. Spring and
autumn are also good times to visit; while winter offers great
Christmas shopping, the city feels more subdued. From June to
August, long light nights mean that socialising goes on
until late.

ANNUAL EVENTS

A year-round programme includes some of the biggest free
festivals in Europe during the summer.

The first fortnight of January sees the Wildlife Photographer
of the Year exhibition at Bristol City Museum and Art Gallery. In
mid-January, the Slapstick Festival celebrates silent comedy in
the Watershed, Arnolfini and Colston Hall. Fairtrade Fortnight
takes place in February.

The Festival of Ideas runs through May at various venues
with lectures and book signings. The second Sunday sees the
Southbank Arts Trail around Southville, Bedminster and Ashton.
Mayfest takes place around the city, centring on the Old Vic.

Bristol Festival of Nature takes place on the second weekend
of June, with lectures, films and animal encounters, plus experts
from the BBC's Natural History Unit.

In July, the Bristol Wine & Food Fair takes place along the
harbourside on the first Friday, then the legendary St Pauls
Carnival on the first Saturday, a riot of colour, music and

multicultural fun. The last weekend sees the Bristol Harbourside Festival with family fun, food, music and acrobatics.

Bristol International Balloon Fiesta takes place at Ashton Court on the second weekend in August.

The first weekend of September sees the Bristol International Festival of Kites and Air Creations at Ashton Court; Bristol Half Marathon takes place on the first Sunday. Doors Open Day allows a glimpse inside historical buildings otherwise closed to the public. The Bristol Festival, with music, art, comedy and culture, takes place on the third weekend around the harbourside area.

In November and December, the Christmas lights go up and shopping venues put on a bit of sparkle. North Bristol and Totterdown have arts trails on separate weekends.

⬤ College Green is a popular spot for picnics in summer

History

Bristol was once England's second city and since its very beginnings, everything has been about the water. Originally known as *Brig-stow*, or the 'place of a bridge', it dates from Anglo-Saxon times when a settlement was established between the Avon and Frome rivers. The oldest area of the city still stands, with the remains of the old city walls and city gate, on Broad Street.

⏶ *The SS Great Britain is Bristol's most popular tourist attraction*

Trade flourished thanks to the waterways, and throughout the Middle Ages wealthy merchants built large houses near the port. Bristol traded with Europe while ships set sail to found colonies in the New World. In 1497, John Cabot set sail in his ship, the *Matthew* (a replica of which is found on the waterfront today), hoping to find a route to the Spice Islands; he actually discovered Newfoundland.

In the 17th century, Methodist leader John Wesley had a chapel erected in Bristol, which remains the oldest Methodist building in the world. The city expanded through the next century with riches transported from around the globe. Bristol has a dark slaving history – in the mid-to-late 18th century, boats made over two thousand slaving voyages and brought an estimated half a million people from Africa in brutal conditions. The slave trade was finally abolished in 1807.

Brunel built Clifton Suspension Bridge, the SS *Great Britain* and Bristol Temple Meads railway station in the 19th century and changed the face of travel in the UK with the Great Western Railway. Trade and commerce declined as other ports gained in prominence.

In more modern times, Bristol became synonymous with the aircraft industry and was heavily bombed in World War II as a result. Many parts of the city still bear the mark of Luftwaffe bombs. Concorde took its first flight here in 1969. Financial services, technology companies and the creative industries thrived from the 1980s, and the city's famous docks, then derelict, moved to Avonmouth, where they have since flourished. Millions of pounds have been spent regenerating the harbourside, which is now a top attraction.

Culture

Bristol isn't defined by stellar galleries or highfalutin orchestras. Culture permeates from grass roots up rather than top down; in fact, it emerges from the streets – graffiti is hugely influential. Uniquely, arts trails take place throughout the year, where people open their homes and display home-grown art to nosey passers-by and neighbours in an excess of community spirit! The Royal West Academy is here and the city counts edgy art college Bower Ashton as a seat of learning.

In the 1990s, Massive Attack, Portishead and Tricky established laid-back trip hop as the Bristol sound, but now you can find gypsy folk, jazz, and a reggae enthusiast and festival favourite in his late 60s, DJ Derek, as signature sounds – anything goes.

TV flourishes in the city, where *Casualty*, *Being Human*, *Skins* and *Mistresses* are all filmed. The BBC's Natural History Unit creates world-leading documentaries here, and Aardman, home of Wallace and Gromit, Morph and Shaun the Sheep, is also based in Bristol.

There isn't space here to cover half of what is going on; suffice it to say that culture is part of the fabric of the city, and to miss it would be to seriously miss out.

▶ *Take a break at one of the many cafés on Park St, the steepest in Bristol*

 # MAKING THE MOST OF
Bristol

Shopping

Bristol's shopping scene is eclectic to say the least, with a blend of designer fashion outlets like Harvey Nichols rubbing shoulders with West Country delis and areas specialising in independent retailers.

There are three main centres: **Cabot Circus**, **Broadmead** and **Cribbs Causeway**. Cabot Circus counts Harvey Nichols and House of Fraser among its designer brands and extends to Quakers Friars, the most luxurious shopping area in the city. Broadmead backs on to it, with plenty of high street stores including Boots, Superdrug, Gap and Debenhams. Out of the city on the M5, Cribbs Causeway has John Lewis, a large Marks & Spencer, DIY superstores and plenty more.

Beyond the chain stores, Bristol has plenty of character. **Park Street** is steep and is full of funky fashion and independent retailers. Stand-out shops are Diana Porter Contemporary Jewellery and the Bristol Guild, an arty interiors shop with a great value café.

Park Street leads up to Clifton **Triangle**, with clothes shops and bakeries thronging with students, and on into **Clifton Village**, with boutiques, interiors shops and upmarket cafés, and also to **Whiteladies Road**, with more designer interiors shops.

Gloucester Road is one of the UK's few shopping streets that still has an independent butcher, baker and hardware store (no candlestick maker, mind), and a good number of greengrocers and independent retailers, including a brew-your-own beer shop.

MARKETS

St Nicholas Markets, or 'St Nick's' to the locals, is a covered market containing a jumble of second-hand bookshops, fabric shops, cafés and pet shops just off Corn Street. Saturday sees the market extend outside the building to Corn Street, with stalls of second-hand clothes, handmade toys and local food. The area also hosts a farmers' market (🕒 09.30–14.30 Wed). 🌐 http://stnicholasmarketbristol.co.uk 🕒 09.30–17.00 Mon–Sat, closed Sun

🔺 *Cabot Circus is the region's undisputed queen of shopping centres*

Eating & drinking

Bristol is a foodie's city, full of great restaurants, markets and delis, not to mention a large number of independent and highly individual cafés, bars and other kinds of eateries.

If you're new to the city, don't miss the region's most celebrated treats: cider and cheese. **The Coronation Tap** in Clifton and **The Apple** on Welsh Back in the city centre are two of the specialist cider pubs. For cheese, you could browse the delis either in **St Nick's Market** or on Gloucester Road, or just choose it as a last course instead of pudding. Somerset Brie and Cheddar are the best buys.

Sustainable, local and organic produce is the flavour of the day round these parts. **Bordeaux Quay** is Bristol's landmark eatery, which has specific environmental concerns, rainwater toilets and a gold rating from the Soil Association. **Pieminister**, on Stokes Croft, makes pies sold throughout the city and is another firm favourite.

But you don't just have to eat British food; freshly made sushi at **Masa** is much favoured by the locals, as is the food at **Thali Café**, which serves Indian thalis in four kitschy restaurants. Baldwin Street has a number of Japanese and Thai restaurants, and there are plenty of Indian restaurants to choose from.

In the summer, Bristol's many parks fill up with picnickers. St Nick's Market offers great takeaway pies, sausage and mash and has plenty of delis to choose from, and it is close to Castle Park; Sainsbury's on Whiteladies Road is the closest supermarket to the Downs.

⬥ The pubs on King Street are the oldest in the city, many with original beams

Entertainment

Bristol is synonymous with a certain type of music, thanks to the sounds of Portishead, Tricky and Massive Attack over a decade ago. These days, you're as likely to hear reggae, pop and jungle as trip hop, but one thing has remained: that laid-back feel.

For more information about the city after dark, pick up a copy of local listings magazine *Venue* or free magazine *The Cut*, or

⬥ *Colston Hall is one of the city's premier live music venues*

visit www.makemeneon.com. Bristol Ticket Shop sells tickets for most events (☎ 0870 444 4400 🕐 www.bristolticketshop.co.uk).

CINEMA

The large **Showcase Cinema De Lux** multiplex is in Cabot Circus and a smaller Odeon cinema is in the town centre. **The Watershed** is Bristol's most acclaimed art house cinema, with foreign films, children's films and themed programmes as well as festivals.

MUSIC & CLUBS

Bristol was voted the UK's most musical city in 2010, based on number of musicians per head of population, and you can find live music every night of the week. **Colston Hall** hosts bands from all over the world, **St George's** has an impressive programme of international classical and folk acts and the **O2 Academy** hosts rock and pop artists fresh from the charts.

The summer sees open-air concerts and festivals in **Queen Square** and at **Ashton Court**. Clubs around the waterfront play pop; Park Street's clubs and bars cater largely for students; and down off Welsh Back, **Thekla**, a club on a boat, hosts some of the hottest indie acts.

THEATRE

Bristol Old Vic is one of the UK's best theatres outside London. It hosts Mayfest, a two-week festival of modern theatre in May – not to be missed – and has regular productions with stellar actors and productions including those from Kneehigh, the renowned Cornish theatre company. Touring musicals and occasional ballet can be found at the **Bristol Hippodrome**.

Sport & relaxation

SPECTATOR SPORTS

The southwest is better known for rugby than its football, but Bristol still sustains two football teams. Bristol City ('The Robins') play in the south of the city in red and white and at time of writing are in the Championship. ⓐ Ashton Gate Stadium ⓣ 0871 222 6666 ⓦ www.bcfc.co.uk

Bristol Rovers ('The Gas'), their arch-rivals, play in the north of the city in blue and white and are in League One. ⓐ Memorial Stadium ⓣ 0117 909 6648 ⓦ www.bristolrovers.co.uk

Bristol Rugby are altogether more successful, however, and play in the RFU Championship. ⓐ Memorial Stadium ⓣ 0117 958 1630 ⓦ www.bristolrugby.co.uk

In summer, international and county cricket games are hosted at the County Ground, where Gloucestershire County Cricket is based. ⓐ Nevil Road ⓣ 0117 910 8000 ⓦ www.gloscricket.co.uk

CYCLING

Bristol is also well known for cycling – despite hills, it has become the UK's premier cycling city (see box, page 36). Cycle hire is available from many places, including:
Blackboy Hill Cycles ⓐ 180 Whiteladies Road ⓣ 0117 973 1420 ⓦ www.blackboycycles.co.uk ⓛ 09.00–17.30 Mon–Sat, 11.00–16.00 Sun
The Ferry Station ⓐ Narrow Quay ⓣ 0117 376 3942 ⓦ http://ferrystation.co.uk

SWIMMING & SPAS

Bristol has a number of swimming pools, the best being at Horfield Leisure Centre beyond Gloucester Road. ⓐ Dorian Road ⓣ 0117 903 1643 ⓦ www.bristol.gov.uk Ⓝ Bus: 75, 75A, 76, 77, 99, 309, 310, 585

Two spas are worth a visit: **The Lido** and **The Relaxation Centre**. The Lido is a renovated Victorian lido with a spa, steam room, sauna and hot tub plus a good restaurant and café. ⓐ Oakfield Place, Clifton ⓣ 0117 933 9530 ⓦ www.lidobristol.com

The Relaxation Centre has outdoor hot tubs, indoor Jacuzzis®, treatment rooms, a flotation tank and a relaxation room. ⓐ 9 All Saints Road, Clifton ⓣ 0117 970 6616 ⓦ www.relaxationcentre.co.uk

🔺 *The small but perfectly formed Lido also has a café overlooking the water*

Accommodation

The vast majority of Bristol's hotels are business-focused and within walking distance of everything. For those staying longer, serviced apartments offer a more home-from-home space; for budget travellers, there are backpacker-style hostels and low-priced hotel chains in the city. Luxury and boutique hotels, however, are few and far between.

Baltic Wharf Caravan Park £ Waterside caravan park in the docklands area near the SS *Great Britain*, open year round. ⓐ Cumberland Road ⓣ 01342 326944 ⓦ www.caravanclub.co.uk ⓔ UKSitesBookingService@caravanclub.co.uk ⓝ Bus: 500, 510

Bristol Youth Hostel £ Fantastic waterfront location in a converted warehouse; bike storage, comfortable lounges and kitchen. ⓐ 14 Narrow Quay ⓣ 0845 371 9726 ⓦ www.yha.org.uk ⓔ Bristol@yha.org.uk ⓝ Bus: 902, 903, 904

Future Inn £ Budget hotel next to Cabot Circus. Free parking in shopping centre car park; weekly jazz club. ⓐ Bond Street South ⓣ 0845 094 5588 ⓦ www.futureinns.co.uk ⓔ reservations.bristol@futureinns.co.uk ⓝ Bus: 8, 9

Premier Inn Haymarket £ Budget skyscraper hotel in the city centre, convenient for Cabot Circus and Broadmead. There is another Premier Inn on King Street. ⓐ The Haymarket ⓣ 0870 238 3307 ⓕ 0117 910 0619 ⓦ www.premierinn.com ⓝ Bus: 8, 9

Rock'n'Bowl Motel £ Budget backpacker accommodation above Bristol's 1950s-style bowling alley, bar and restaurant. Twin rooms plus six-, eight-, ten- and twelve-bed dorms. 🅐 22 Nelson Street 🕾 0117 929 4861 🅦 www.rocknbowlmotel.com 🅔 bookings@rocknbowlmotel.com Ⓝ Bus: 8, 9

The Avon Gorge Hotel ££ This hotel undoubtedly offers the best views of Clifton Suspension Bridge plus a great outdoors drinking and dining area. It is popular with university visitors and wedding parties. 🅐 Sion Hill, Clifton 🕾 0117 973 8955 🅦 www.theavongorge.com 🅔 rooms@theavongorge.com Ⓝ Bus: 8, 9

Berkeley Square Hotel ££ Boutique hotel in the heart of Clifton, well placed for the university. 🅐 15 Berkeley Square 🕾 0117 925 4000 🅦 www.cliftonhotels.com Ⓝ Bus: 8, 9

The Bristol Hotel ££ Stylish boutique hotel overlooking the water in the city centre; great bar and popular River Grille restaurant. 🅐 Prince Street 🕾 0117 923 0333 🅦 www.doylecollection.com 🅔 bristol@doylecollection.com Ⓝ Bus: 902, 903, 904

City Inn ££ Smart, modern business hotel near Temple Meads station with an award-winning bistro, City Café. iMac laptops and free wi-fi. 🅐 Temple Way 🕾 0117 925 1001 🅦 www.cityinn.com 🅔 Bristol.reservations@cityinn.com Ⓝ Bus: 8, 9

The Grand Hotel ££ Stylish, affordable hotel near St Nick's Market in the heart of Bristol; free car park. ⓐ Broad Street ⓣ 0871 376 9042 ⓕ 0871 376 9142 ⓦ www.thistle.com ⓝ Bus: 1, 51, 54, X39

Holiday Inn Express ££ One of the chain's business- and wallet-friendly hotels, close to the station and business district. ⓐ South End, Temple Gate House ⓣ 0117 930 4800 ⓦ www.hiexpress.co.uk ⓔ Bristol@morethanhotels.com ⓝ Bus: 8, 9

Mercure Brigstow Hotel ££ Modern waterfront hotel with bar, restaurant and access to nearby gym. ⓐ 5–7 Welsh Back ⓣ 0117 929 1030 ⓦ www.mercure.com ⓔ H6548@accor.com ⓝ Bus: X27

Mercure Holland House Hotel & Spa ££ A short walk from Temple Meads station, this four-star accommodation is Bristol's only spa hotel. ⓐ Redcliffe Hill ⓣ 0117 968 9900 ⓦ www.mercure.com ⓔ H6698@accor.com ⓝ Bus: 902, 903, 904

Novotel Bristol Centre ££ Comfortable business-style hotel within five minutes' walk of Temple Meads station. ⓐ Victoria Street ⓣ 0117 976 9988 ⓦ www.novotel.com ⓔ H5622@accor.com ⓝ Bus: 8, 9

Portland Apartments ££ Boutique serviced apartments near Cabot Circus and Whiteladies Road and in the city centre. Weekly stays preferred. ⓐ 26 Portland Square ⓣ 0117 924 9111

Ⓦ www.portlandapartments.co.uk
Ⓔ reservations@portlandapartments.co.uk
Ⓝ Bus: 8, 9, X23, X73 (alight at House of Fraser)

Radisson Blu ££ Bristol's newest hotel is in the city centre overlooking the waterfront, with an Italian restaurant, health club and impressive views. Ⓐ Broad Quay ⓣ 0117 934 9500
Ⓦ www.radissonblu.co.uk/hotel-bristol
Ⓔ info.bristol@radissonblu.com
Ⓝ Any city-centre-bound bus, 8, 9 (alight at Hippodrome)

SACO Apartments ££ Modern serviced apartments, central location beside Bristol Bridge and on Victoria Street.
Ⓐ West India House and Victoria Street ⓣ 0845 122 0405
Ⓦ www.sacoapartments.co.uk Ⓔ info@sacoapartments.co.uk
Ⓝ Bus: 902, 903, 904
ⓘ Breakfast not included

Bristol Marriott Royal Hotel ££–£££ Landmark hotel next to Bristol Cathedral with all mod cons, some four-poster-beds, pool, leisure club, two restaurants and a Champagne Bar.
Ⓐ College Green ⓣ 0117 925 5100 ⓕ 0117 925 1515
Ⓦ www.marriott.co.uk Ⓝ Bus: 1, 8, 9, 40, 41

Hotel du Vin £££ Bristol's finest hotel has a superb bistro/restaurant and bar and is close to the city centre and waterfront. Ⓐ The Sugar House, Narrow Lewins Mead
ⓣ 0117 925 5577 ⓕ 0117 910 5408 Ⓦ www.hotelduvin.com
Ⓝ Bus: 8, 9 (alight at Hippodrome)

THE BEST OF BRISTOL

Take your time, enjoy Bristol's laid-back atmosphere and don't try to fit in too much.

TOP 10 ATTRACTIONS

- **Brunel's Clifton Suspension Bridge** Take a walk over this bridge, as striking today as it was when it opened in 1864 (see page 68).

- **SS _Great Britain_** Brunel's other great masterpiece was the world's first great ocean-going liner (see page 58).

- **M Shed** Opening in 2011, this stands to be the city's showpiece museum on the harbourside, full of interactive exhibits (see pages 55–6).

- **Ashton Court** An afternoon spent at leisure here can't be missed, whether you visit the house, the woods, the pitch and putt course or the deer park (see page 66).

- **Banksy trail** Spot some well-known pieces of art around the city without setting foot inside a gallery (see page 74).

- **The Lido** Take a dip in this revamped Victorian lido in Clifton (see page 69).

- **Bristol's ferries** See the historic harbourside from the water (see page 91).

- **On two wheels** Hire a bike and find out why Bristol has been named the UK's foremost cycling city (see page 36).

- **Theatres** Find a new perspective on performance art at Mayfest or the Old Vic (see pages 44–6).

- **Festivals** Make time to visit one of Bristol's many festivals. The city has something going on every month, from arts trails to hot air balloon and kite festivals (see pages 8–9).

Brunel's famous suspension bridge, now one of Bristol's most recognisable features

Suggested itineraries

HALF-DAY: BRISTOL IN A HURRY

Don't rush – that's not the Bristol way. Take a stroll down around the reinvigorated waterfront area, where you'll find the Arnolfini contemporary art gallery, the M Shed (from 2011), the Watershed art-house cinema, the Visitor Information Centre and plenty of boats and cafés to keep you amused. From this viewpoint, you'll be able to see the suspension bridge in Clifton and the coloured houses of Hotwells and Totterdown on the hills all around. To cover ground more quickly, take a ferry boat ride along the river. Then round your day off with a pint of West Country cider at the Apple bar, a boat floating on the river.

1 DAY: TIME TO SEE A LITTLE MORE

Hire a bike and explore the city. Bristol's hilly topography isn't really suited to cycling, but everybody seems to do it anyway. Once you've been along the waterfront, push your bike up Park Street and investigate Clifton. From here you can find the suspension bridge, the Downs and the Observatory, and some fantastic views of the Avon Gorge. Stop for a breather and a drink at the Avon Gorge Hotel. Clifton has plenty of boutiques where you can lose yourself for the afternoon, and cafés, bars and restaurants open into the night.

2–3 DAYS & LONGER: SHORT CITY BREAK

If you have a weekend or more, you can take in all the top ten attractions of the city. While you're in Clifton, walk over the suspension bridge and spend an afternoon in Ashton Court.

And if it's all getting too much for you, relax at the Lido or the Relaxation Centre, with their spas, saunas and steam rooms. Culture fans should take in a play at the Old Vic. And art fans should be able to find a Banksy or ten in the city – try the Easton Banksy trail if you love your graffiti, or wander up Park Street and spot his recent addition. You could also spend a few days in Bath and take drives out to the Somerset countryside.

Lazy summer days can be spent relaxing at Ashton Court

Something for nothing

You don't need to spend money to have a good time. Start off by taking a walk along the harbourside. This will take you past the Arnolfini (see pages 58–9), a free modern art gallery, and across the bridge to M Shed (opening in 2011) (see pages 55–6). The Bristol City Museum and Art Gallery (see pages 70–71) and Royal West of England Academy (RWA) (see page 71), at the top of Park Street, are also free. History buffs can enjoy Brunel's engineering brilliance at Clifton Suspension Bridge (see page 68) and Bristol Temple Meads (see page 42).

Events and festivals happen nearly every month throughout the year and regular summer events are among the largest free festivals in Europe. These include the Balloon Fiesta, the Bristol Harbour Festival and the International Kite Festival (see pages 8–9). Queen Square (see pages 57–8), in summer, also hosts free jazz concerts and occasional cinema screenings. And the country estate of Ashton Court (see page 66), just across the suspension bridge, is also free to visit.

The tourist office website (ⓦ http://visitbristol.co.uk) has MP3 walking routes for the city that you can download and follow for nowt; you can choose from The Bristol Quayside Adventure, The Brunel Mile, The Heritage Trail, The Churches Trail, The Slave Trade Trail or The Literary Trail.

When it rains

It does rain in Bristol and, despite being in the temperate southwest, it can be cold in winter months. What to do? Head inside for the city's best tourist attractions. Millennium Square has plenty of family-orientated offerings, including At-Bristol, an IMAX cinema and Blue Reef aquarium. The city's art galleries and museums, including the Red House, Arnolfini gallery and City Museum and Art Gallery, are all free and worth a visit. The Watershed, Old Vic, Colston Hall, Hippodrome, St George's and other cultural venues are also worth checking out. Or you could visit Bristol Zoo, most of which is covered.

If you're in the mood for shopping, Cabot Circus is under cover and boasts a multiplex cinema with director's box options for serious film buffs, alongside restaurants, cafés and shops. And if the rain hasn't dampened your spirits for exploring the wider city and seeing the sights, City Sightseeing tours, on red buses, will take you round the top picks of the city without exposing you to the rain.

On arrival

Most UK visitors arrive by rail, road or coach and it's easy to find your way around. If you arrive at Bristol Airport, buses, car hire and taxi services are also easy to negotiate.

ARRIVING
By air
Bristol's small, one-terminal international airport, 13 km (8 miles) south of the city, has cafés, a small array of shops, plus car hire desks. To reach the city centre, you need to drive, hire a car, or take a taxi or bus.

By rail
There's a sense of history as you arrive at Temple Meads, the oldest and largest railway station in the UK. The station is busy with 15 platforms and is the main travel hub to the West Country.

In terms of facilities, a handful of shops and cafés and two ATMs are on the railway side. If you need cash be sure to get it here – before the automated ticket barriers – as there is no ATM on the other side or anywhere near the station.

Outside there is a taxi rank and buses run from the right-hand side up to Clifton and into the city centre. The Bristol Flyer coach runs from the left-hand side. Temple Meads is central and within walking distance of a number of hotels, for example City Inn, but those staying near the waterfront and away from the immediate area should take a taxi. Two key buses, the 8 and 9, run in a loop through the city centre to Clifton and Redland and back to the station.

By road

Arriving by car should be no problem if you have satnav or know where you're going. If you don't – beware! Central Bristol can be tricky to negotiate, full of traffic, bikes and one-way systems. Check with your hotel or lodgings before setting off to get some good navigational advice.

The main hazards are cyclists, of whom there are many, and parking inspectors. Most of the city centre has permit or meter parking and you need to carry change for these. Parking inspectors show no mercy. After arrival, you will probably find it easier to explore on foot or by bike or public transport rather than by car.

FINDING YOUR FEET

As with every major UK city, Bristol has crime problems, so don't flaunt your jewellery, hold on to your handbag and don't wander down ill-lit alleys after dark.

The city is a patchwork of villages and some are more desirable than others; the areas of Bedminster, St Pauls and Easton are best avoided after dark. However, if you stick to well-trodden paths in the city centre you shouldn't have any trouble.

ORIENTATION

In general, this is an easy city to navigate as the centre is fairly compact. It's all arranged around the harbourside, which works as an orientation point; uphill you'll find Clifton and the West End and away from it you'll find the city centre spreading through Broadmead and Cabot Circus.

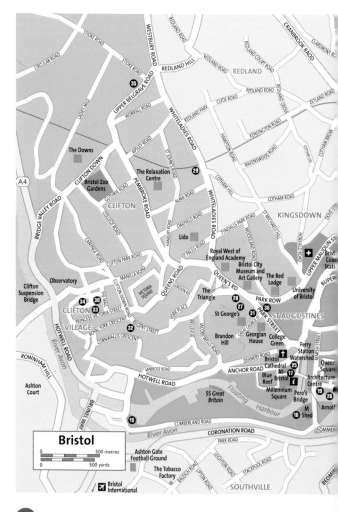

Bristol

0 — 500 metres
0 — 500 yards

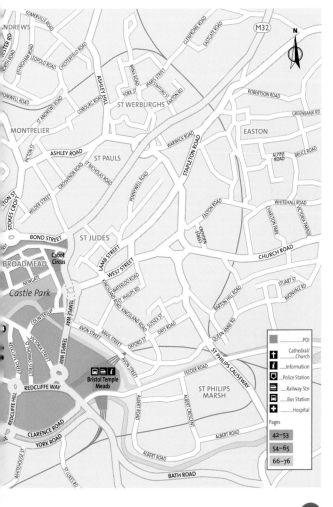

35

GETTING AROUND

Nearly 10 per cent of Bristolians cycle to work, and you can't blame them as traffic jams increase around rush hour, buses are expensive and it is hard to park. From the centre, you can walk nearly everywhere but cycling is also a great way to see the city – make sure you secure your bike firmly to a bike rack when you leave it. Cycle crime is rife.

The bus network is patchy and expensive; the 8 and 9 buses run in a loop around the city centre and are all you really need if

CYCLING IN BRISTOL

Since 2009, Bristol has been the UK's first cycling city. There's still a long way to go before there are safe bike lanes in the city centre, but it's a reflection of the way Bristol sees itself – green, healthy and sustainable. You can hire a bike from the following:

Blackboy Hill Cycles ⓐ 180 Whiteladies Road ⓣ 0117 973 1420 ⓦ www.blackboycycles.co.uk

The Ferry Station ⓐ Narrow Quay ⓣ 0117 376 3942 ⓦ http://ferrystation.co.uk

Hourbike (hourly hire) ⓐ Central locations ⓦ www.hourbike.com

Better by Bike (ⓦ www.betterbybike.co.uk) has maps and routes for Bristol and beyond. Cycling charity **Sustrans** (ⓦ www.sustrans.org.uk) is based in the city and has long-distance routes, holidays and tips for everyone.

you don't want to walk but the City Sightseeing bus works out as a better-value option (see page 91 for details). The long-distance Coach Station is on Marlborough Street, but most local buses stop elsewhere around the centre.

To visit Somerset's attractions, having a car really helps; the few bus services and rail links are slow, infrequent and inflexible. Visiting Bath, however, is easiest on public transport, on either the slow bus or the regular 15-minute train from Temple Meads.

CAR HIRE

Car hire desks at the airport can help with a car for your stay; car hire in town is a bit hit and miss. **Holiday Autos** compares

⬤ *Cycling is a convenient way to get around*

best-value options; prices start at around £35 per day.

Ⓦ www.holidayautos.co.uk

Avis ⓐ Rupert Street ⓣ 0844 544 6043 Ⓦ www.avis.co.uk

Budget ⓐ Fairfax Street ⓣ 0117 316 9090 Ⓦ www.budget.co.uk

Europcar ⓐ Berkeley Place, Jacob's Wells Road, Clifton

ⓣ 0117 925 3839 Ⓦ www.europcar.co.uk

If you really want to soak up the West Country atmosphere in style and explore Somerset and surrounding counties, you could hire a campervan. **The Bristol Camper Company** arranges pick-ups at the airport or delivery into the city and costs from £325 for three days. ⓐ Acacia Farm, Bristol Road, Rooksbridge

ⓣ 0845 467 4147 Ⓦ www.thebristolcampercompany.co.uk

ⓔ info@thebristolcampercompany.co.uk

HOT-AIR BALLOONS

Take to the skies – Bristol is the UK capital of hot-air ballooning and you can take a three- to four-hour trip starting at dawn or a few hours before sunset, with views over the surrounding countryside, Bath and south Wales.

Bailey Balloons ⓐ 44 Ham Green ⓣ 01275 375300

Ⓦ www.baileyballoons.co.uk ⓔ info@baileyballoons.co.uk

ⓛ All year; main season Mar–Nov

Bristol Balloons ⓐ Coronation Road ⓣ 0117 963 7858

Ⓦ www.bristolballoons.co.uk ⓛ Apr–Oct

❱ *Water fountains by the Hippodrome*

THE CITY OF
Bristol

Introduction to city areas

The central area of Bristol breaks down into the **city centre**, where you can still see the old city wall with portcullis channels; the historic **harbourside and waterfront**, newly rebuilt with shiny apartments in the old warehouse buildings as well as a brand new landmark museum opening in 2011; and **Clifton and the West End**, the city's most refined address, with beautiful architecture, hill views and green spaces, and Brunel's famous Clifton Suspension Bridge. Within these three areas you'll find Bristol's top cultural attractions, as well as shops and markets, bars and cafés, restaurants, parks and even a country estate.

Explore each area by foot – most attractions in the city centre are within easy walking distance. The harbourside area particularly lends itself to a gentle stroll alongside moored houseboats and ferries; the walk up to Clifton from the centre is worth it just for the view from Cabot Tower on Brandon Hill.

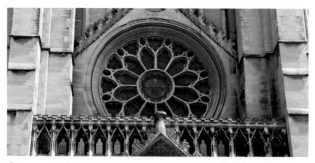

● *Bristol Cathedral has features dating back to the 12th century*

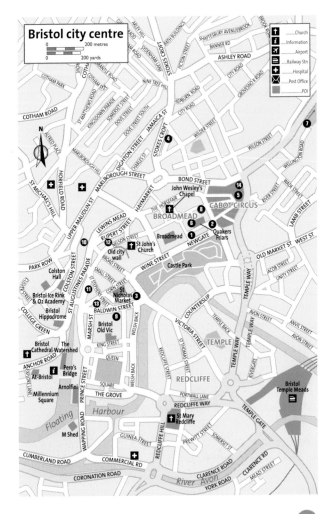

THE CITY

City centre

Shopping and entertainment are the key attractions for visitors in the city centre; it's where you'll find the showpiece shopping centre **Cabot Circus**, as well as a number of historic sights, pubs with literary heritage and the stunning **Old Vic** theatre.

SIGHTS & ATTRACTIONS

Bristol Ice Rink
Ice skating, ice karting and ice hockey are three of the attractions on offer at this ice rink above the O2 Academy on Frogmore Street. ⓐ Frogmore Street ❶ 0117 929 2148 ⓦ http://jnlbristol.co.uk ❶ 10.00–22.30 daily
❶ Admission charge

Bristol Temple Meads
The Great Western Railway terminus at Bristol Temple Meads is one of Brunel's greatest achievements, with an impressive three-storey Bath stone entrance designed to recall a Tudor mansion. It was completed in 1841, the year that the London–Bristol route opened, and was at that time the first true railway terminus where people and trains were beneath the same roof.
ⓐ Station Approach, Temple Meads

Castle Park
This central park is the biggest green space in the city centre and popular for picnics in the summer (St Nick's Market is the best place to pick up food nearby). On an ancient riverside site, it

has important archaeological remains with the remnants of a great medieval castle, built by the Normans and demolished by Oliver Cromwell in 1650, and St Peter's Church, which was bombed in World War II. Next to the church, you'll find a small sensory herb garden and seven silver birch trees in honour of the seven beaches of the D-Day landings. ⓐ Newgate ⓣ 0117 922 3719 ⓔ bristolparks@bristol.gov.uk

John Wesley's Chapel

John Wesley's Chapel is the oldest Methodist building in the world. The chapel has been restored and retains wooden pews and galleries from 1748. Upstairs there is an MLA-accredited museum telling the story of Wesley's life with some personal items. ⓐ 36 The Horsefair ⓣ 0117 926 4740 ⓦ www.newroombristol.org.uk ⓛ 10.00–16.00 Mon–Sat, closed Sun

Old city wall

Bristol was once surrounded by a city wall and small portions of it remain. St John's Gate, the last remaining part, was a fortified gateway and can be seen in Broad Street. The legendary founders of Bristol, Brennus and Belinus, are immortalised in the niches. You can still see portcullis channels within the arch. St John's Church next to it was built at the end of the 14th century.

St Mary Redcliffe

The Gothic spire of St Mary Redcliffe houses a wealth of 18th-century ironwork and stained glass and was once referred to by Elizabeth I as 'The fairest, goodliest and most famous

⬤ *St Mary Redcliffe's spire makes it the tallest building in Bristol*

parish church in England'. The church overlooks the floating harbour and was at the heart of Bristol's shipping industry, when merchants would begin and end their journeys here.
ⓐ Redcliffe Way ⓣ 0117 929 1487 ⓦ www.stmaryredcliffe.co.uk
ⓛ 08.20–17.00 daily

CULTURE

Bristol Hippodrome

This city centre venue hosts touring Lloyd Webber musicals, ballet, big name comedians, occasional opera and big budget touring productions from the West End. ⓐ 10 Saint Augustine's Parade ⓣ 0844 847 2341 ⓦ www.bristolhippodrome.org.uk

Bristol Old Vic

The city's oldest theatre is home to its most cutting-edge, modern drama scene. Its theatre school, set up by Laurence Olivier in 1946, has alumni including Daniel Day-Lewis, Miranda Richardson and Jeremy Irons. It now offers both traditional format theatre in its historic building, dating to 1766, and experiential performances, festivals, family theatre, one-off events and the superb Mayfest, a two-week festival of experimental theatre. **ⓐ** King Street **ⓣ** 0117 949 3993 **ⓦ** www.bristololdvic.org.uk **ⓔ** explore@bristol-old-vic.co.uk **ⓘ** Backstage tours incur a small charge

Colston Hall

The gilded, sweeping modern wing of Colston Hall is worth visiting in itself; this concert hall hosts some of the very best music in the city, from classical to pop and rock, with a particular line in world music. Its h-bar bistro and terrace bar are a delight (book ahead for weekend dinners) and as well as lunchtime and evening concerts, there are pre-concert talks and regular after-show parties. **ⓐ** Colston Street **ⓣ** 0117 922 3686 **ⓦ** www.colstonhall.org **ⓔ** enews@colstonhall.org

The O2 Academy

Bristol's O2 Academy attracts big names from the charts touring the UK and has a regular indie event on a Saturday night. **ⓐ** Frogmore Street **ⓣ** 0844 477 2000 **ⓦ** www.o2academybristol.co.uk

The Tobacco Factory

One of the city's former tobacco factories, south of the river in
Southville, has been south Bristol's premier arts and culture
destination for over ten years. The theatre has a regular
Shakespeare season and shows avant-garde theatre, puppetry
and festivals as well as hosting big name comedians on
nationwide tours. The bar/restaurant downstairs is popular
in its own right. ⓐ North Street/Raleigh Road, Southville
ⓣ 0117 902 0344 ⓦ www.tobaccofactorytheatre.com
ⓝ Bus: 25 from the city centre stops outside

🔺 *The Old Vic shows plays by innovative new writers as well as reworked classics*

RETAIL THERAPY

The city centre is the place to shop if you're looking for big brand international designers or high street shops.

Broadmead Broadmead grew up as a shopping centre in post-war Bristol, which accounts for its utilitarian and concrete architecture. Since Cabot Circus opened, it has looked fairly dowdy, but it's still the best place in the heart of the city to find high street shops that you really need: opticians, pharmacists, Marks & Spencer and a small supermarket.
Ⓦ www.bristolbroadmead.co.uk Ⓛ 09.00–18.00 Mon–Sat, 11.00–17.00 Sun

Cabot Circus Bristol's newest shopping centre, opened at the end of 2009, is a glittering celebration of designer labels and high street fashion and has some interesting entertainment options, including a Cinema De Lux with 13 screens and Jungle Rumble, an indoor Adventure Golf course with its own volcano. The glass roof means that you don't have to brave the city streets in wet weather. Shops include Urban Outfitters, House of Fraser, Hollister and Dwell; the centre's second-floor eateries include Tampopo, Café Rouge, Giraffe and Patisserie Valerie.
Ⓣ 0117 952 9360 Ⓦ www.cabotcircus.com Ⓛ 10.00–20.00 Mon–Sat, 11.00–17.00 Sun, 10.00–18.00 Bank Holidays
ⓘ Restaurants and cinema open later

Quakers Friars The upmarket arm of Cabot Circus, Quakers Friars is outdoor and arranged around a central square with a fountain. Brasserie Blanc is its centrepoint, housed in a fabulous former Georgian Quaker meeting hall with two medieval halls behind it. They were built as a monastery in the 13th and 14th centuries and afterwards used by Bristol's bakers and cutlers as guildhalls – what could be more appropriate? Around it you'll find the cream of the city's upmarket labels, including Harvey Nichols, Hugo Boss and Apple. ☎ 0117 952 9360 ⓦ www.cabotcircus.com 🕐 10.00–20.00 Mon–Sat, 11.00–17.00 Sun, 10.00–18.00 Bank Holidays ❗ Restaurants open later

St Nicholas Markets 'St Nicks', as it's known to locals, has been named one of the ten best markets in the UK; it contains

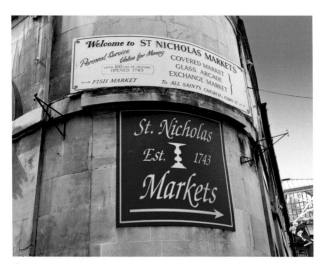

🔻 *You can buy just about anything at this permanent market*

second-hand bookshops, fabric shops, cafés and pet shops plus a large number of independent retailers. Saturday sees the market extend outside the building to Corn Street, with stalls of second-hand clothes, handmade toys and local food. The area also hosts a farmers' market (🕒 09.30–14.30 Wed). It's the best place nearby to grab a coffee and watch the world go by. 🌐 http://stnicholasmarketbristol.co.uk 🕒 09.30–17.00 Mon–Sat, closed Sun

TAKING A BREAK

Chandos Deli £ ❶ Independent and wildly successful southwest deli chain selling soup and sandwiches, charcuterie, cheese and plenty more, with free tasters. 🅰 Quakers Friars ☎ 0117 974 3275 🌐 www.chandosdeli.com 🕒 09.00–17.00 Mon, 08.30–19.00 Tues–Fri, 09.00–17.30 Sat, 10.00–16.00 Sun

Harvey Nichols £ ❷ The Second Floor restaurant is chic, golden-hued and not really very 'Bristol' – in that you feel like you should dress up to eat here. Expect anything from visiting Michelin-starred chefs in the restaurant to fancy cupcakes and serious cocktails in the bijou bar. Great value set menus – you won't believe it. 🅰 Philadelphia Street, Quakers Friars ☎ 0117 916 8898 🌐 www.harveynichols.com 🕒 10.00–17.30 Mon, 10.00–22.00 Tues–Sat, 11.00–16.00 Sun

The Old Fishmarket £ ❸ Pub with fantastic Thai food. Unpretentious, great value and plenty of beer to wash it all down with. 🅰 59–63 Baldwin Street ☎ 0117 921 1515

Pieminister £ ❹ Local independent café celebrating the art of pie making just off the city centre. Worth the walk!
ⓐ 24 Stokes Croft; also in St Nick's Market ☏ 0117 942 9372
ⓦ www.pieminister.co.uk ⏰ 11.00–19.00 Mon–Sat, 11.00–17.00 Sun

Tampopo £ ❺ Next to Cabot Circus' Cinema De Lux, this fusion restaurant serves up tasty flavours from all over the Far East.
ⓐ Level 3, Cabot Circus ☏ 0117 927 7008 ⓦ www.tampopo.co.uk
⏰ 12.00–23.00 Mon–Sat, 12.00–22.00 Sun

Brasserie Blanc ££ ❻ Celebrated chef Raymond Blanc's easy-dining French brasserie is housed in architectural splendour.
ⓐ Quakers Friars ☏ 0117 910 2410 ⓦ www.brasserieblanc.com
ⓔ bristol@brasserieblanc.com ⏰ 10.00–22.00 Mon–Thur, 10.00–22.30 Fri & Sat, 10.00–21.00 Sun

Café Maitreya ££ ❼ Bristol's award-winning Café Maitreya deserves a special mention – it is regularly voted the UK's top vegetarian restaurant. It's out of the city centre in Easton (take a taxi) and serves elegant and inventive spins on veggie cuisine.
ⓐ 89 St Mark's Road, Easton ☏ 0117 951 0100
ⓦ www.cafemaitreya.co.uk

Carluccios ££ ❽ Casual Italian café in the corner of Quakers Friars. Outdoor seating in good weather; small deli attached.
ⓐ Quakers Friars ☏ 0117 933 8538 ⓦ www.carluccios.com
⏰ 08.00–23.00 Mon–Sat, 10.00–22.30 Sun

Masa ££ ❾ Japanese restaurant with sushi freshly made in front of your eyes, Teppanyaki-style eating and a sushi conveyor belt. The real deal. ⓐ 42–46 Baldwin Street ❶ 0117 929 3888 ⓦ www.masajapaneserestaurant.com

Hotel du Vin £££ ❿ Classy bistro serving classic European cuisine in a French-styled dining room with adjacent bar and cigar booth. The best restaurant in Bristol. ⓐ The Sugar House, Narrow Lewins Mead ❶ 0117 925 5577 ❶ 0117 910 5408 ⓦ www.hotelduvin.com ❶ Daily for breakfast, lunch and dinner at varying times

🔺 *The Mall in Broadmead has over 80 shops*

AFTER DARK

Central Bristol has cinemas, music and entertainment; the best bars are elsewhere.

King Street King Street borders the waterfront area and is full of pubs. **The Old Duke** plays jazz on a Sunday and is small but fun; **The Llandoger Trow**, a Grade II listed building, dates back to 1664 and despite being bombed in World War II, still retains original features. Tradition has it that Robert Louis Stevenson used it as the inspiration for the Admiral Benbow in *Treasure Island* and that Daniel Defoe met Alexander Selkirk, who inspired Robinson Crusoe, here. **The Royal Navy Volunteer** is another

⬥ Bowl, sing or dance at The Lanes

historical pub on the street, dating to the 17th century. In good weather, tables are put out on the street and all the pubs mingle together.

Karaoke Me ⑪ Japanese-style booths, fancy dress and waiter service. Thank goodness all rooms are soundproofed! Book by the hour. ⓐ 12 St Stephens Street ⓣ 0117 376 3100 ⓦ www.karaoke-me.co.uk ⓛ 18.00–24.00 Mon–Wed, 18.00–01.00 Thur, 18.00–02.00 Fri & Sat, closed Sun

The Lanes ⑫ This 1950s-style retro bowling alley is great fun, with a traditional-style diner, regular themed nights, karaoke in a private booth and a dancefloor on a Saturday night. Upstairs there's a comedy club and occasional cinema screenings. ⓐ 22 Nelson Street ⓣ 0117 325 1979 ⓦ www.thelanesbristol.co.uk ❶ No under-18s after 16.00

Mr Wolfs ⑬ Independent bar/club/noodle bar favoured by Bristol music fans in the know. It's a bit shabby but very cool, bringing together live music, a local arty crowd and graffiti artists. The club's eclectic DJs play anything from disco to reggae. ⓐ 33 St Stephens Street ⓣ 0117 927 3221 ⓦ www.mrwolfs.com

Showcase Cinema De Lux ⑭ Slap bang in the centre of the city, this 13-screen cinema shows blockbusters and the like, with a special director's box with reclining leather chairs, cocktail lounge and order-from-your-seat facilities. ⓐ Level 3, Cabot Circus ⓣ 0871 220 1000 ⓦ www.cinemadelux.co.uk

Harbourside & waterfront

Bristol's historic harbourside and waterfront areas are the key draw in the city. Take a walk around and explore the history with the help of a pirate friend (see page 57); relax and watch the world go by at one of the many waterfront cafés and bars, or visit the city's newest museum, M Shed, when it opens in 2011, for a unique insight into Bristol's history, culture and lifestyle.

SIGHTS & ATTRACTIONS

The sights of the boats and ferries along the water's edge might be enough; if you want more, you'll find museums, galleries and plenty for kids.

Architecture Centre

Small museum showcasing architecture and sustainability on the first floor, with a fun shop selling quirky children's toys, designer interiors items and handmade jewellery on the ground floor. ⓐ Narrow Quay ① 0117 922 1540 ⓦ www.architecturecentre.co.uk ⓒ 11.00–17.00 Tues–Fri, 12.00–17.00 Sat & Sun, closed Mon

At-Bristol

At-Bristol, often styled as '@Bristol', is one of the UK's biggest and most interactive science centres and a great option for families, with over 300 hands-on exhibits and a Planetarium. Live science shows are full of lively demos and experiments and the Animate it! Gallery gives your nippers a chance to try their

luck at being animators for the day, with input from locals
Aardman Animation. ⓐ Anchor Road ⓣ 0845 345 1235
ⓦ www.at-bristol.org.uk ⓛ 10.00–17.00 Mon–Fri, 10.00–18.00
Sat, Sun & school holidays ⓘ Admission charge

Blue Reef

The Blue Reef aquarium, in Millennium Square, is one of the
city's newest attractions. In it you can visit the underwater
gardens of the Med, see the most stunning species from around
the British coast, such as conger eels and wolf fish, and spot
some (small) sharks. It's also the home of Millennium Square's
IMAX 3D cinema, well worth a visit for its underwater journey.
ⓐ Anchor Road ⓣ 0117 929 8929
ⓦ www.bluereefaquarium.co.uk ⓛ 10.00–17.00 Mon–Fri,
10.00–18.00 Sat–Sun & school holidays ⓝ Bus: 8 or 9 to
College Green then walk down to the harbourside
ⓘ Admission charge, entry to IMAX included in price

Bristol Visitor Information Centre

Bristol's main information centre is on the waterside and
offers accommodation booking, tickets and general advice.
You can buy souvenirs and uniquely there is a display of
local art for sale too. ⓐ E-Shed, Canons Road
ⓣ 0333 321 0101 ⓦ http://visitbristol.co.uk
ⓔ ticharbourside@destinationbristol.co.uk ⓛ 10.00–17.00 daily

M Shed

Bristol's brand new museum, opening in spring 2011, is set to
bring the best of the city's culture and history to life, with

interactive exhibitions and displays on everything from history to reggae. The museum is set in a former 1950s transit shed with floor-to-ceiling windows, a café, and three galleries on People, Place and Living Bristol, including anything from Concorde to the Blitz and the Beatles playing at Colston Hall. As a living museum, it will also seek your opinion on the city, with visitor and local comments going forward to fuel future exhibits. Well worth a visit. ⓐ Princes Wharf ⓦ www.mshed.org ⓛ Please consult the website for details of opening hours as they were not available at the time of writing

🔺 *Millennium Square with the IMAX theatre in the background*

Millennium Square

This public space just off the waterfront and beside At-Bristol is modern and fresh, featuring waterfalls and fountains as well as a statue of Cary Grant, one of the city's most famous sons.

Pero's Bridge

This pedestrian bridge, built in 1999, links Queen Square and Millennium Square and has distinctive horns which work as cantilevers when the bridge lifts for large boats. It's named after Pero, a slave of the merchant John Pinney, who arrived in the city from Nevis in the Caribbean in 1783.

Pirate walks

Why are pirates called pirates? Because they *aaaaaargh*. Get yourself in the mood for pirates with Peter the Pirate's walks around the waterside. Starting at the Black Beetle near Millennium Square, his hour-long wanderings around the water take in Bristol's slave trail, pirate haunts, Blackbeard's lair, the medieval quays and a search for Long John Silver's treasure chest. Great fun. ☎ 07950 566483 Ⓦ www.piratewalks.co.uk ⓔ peterthepirate@hotmail.com 🕑 14.00 Sat & Sun ❶ Admission charge

Queen Square

Queen Square, surrounded by grand Georgian buildings, is one of Bristol's best open spaces. In the summer, jazz festivals take place as well as outdoor Shakespeare performances and various weekend festivals, and at other times, it is popular with picnickers and sunbathers. The square dates from 1699 and was named for Queen Anne; the statue in the centre remembers William III.

SS *Great Britain*

Isambard Kingdom Brunel's SS *Great Britain* was the first ocean-going liner in the world, launched in 1843. At this time, it was the largest vessel afloat in the world, carrying 360 passengers and 120 crew, and sailed a route from Liverpool to New York. When its owners went out of business in 1846 after the ship ran aground in Ireland, it carried immigrants to Australia for 35 years, before being retired to the Falkland Islands and used as a warehouse, quarantine ship and coal scuttle. There were huge celebrations in Bristol in 1970 when it was returned to the city's dry dock. The ship has been transformed into an award-winning visitor attraction, offering a chance to see what it was like to travel both as a passenger and as crew – with realistic sounds and smells. ⓐ Great Western Dockyard ❶ 0117 926 0680 ⓦ www.ssgreatbritain.org ⓛ Daily 10.00–17.30 (Apr–Oct); 10.00–16.30 (Nov–Mar) ❶ Admission charge

CULTURE

The Arnolfini and Watershed are the leading lights in the city's contemporary scene.

Arnolfini

Bristol's premier contemporary art gallery is strangely patchy, given the artistic diversity in the city, and attracts touring international exhibitions, UK artists and abstract installations.

There is a spring poetry festival and live modern dance shows as well as a small art house cinema. Perhaps the biggest draw is its small café-bar and its superlative bookshop.

ⓐ Narrow Quay ⓣ 0117 917 2300 ⓦ www.arnolfini.org.uk
ⓔ boxoffice@arnolfini.org.uk ⓛ 11.00–18.00 Tues–Sun & Bank Holiday Mon, closed Mon

The Watershed

This thriving art-house cinema on the waterfront shows the best independent films in the city, with regular talks and festivals. The café-bar has free wi-fi, serves organic food and drink and is always full of interesting people. ⓐ Canons Road
ⓣ 0117 927 5100 ⓦ www.watershed.co.uk

🔺 With exhibitions, films and festivals, Arnolfini is a premier centre for contemporary art

RETAIL THERAPY

Being so close to the city centre and Park Street shops, this is an area where you'll need to break out the plastic.

Arnolfini bookshop Arnolfini's art bookshop is widely regarded as one of the best in the UK. ⓐ Narrow Quay ⓣ 0117 917 2300 ⓦ www.arnolfini.org.uk ⓛ 11.00–18.00 Tues, 11.00–20.00 Wed–Sat, 11.00–19.00 Sun, closed Mon

TAKING A BREAK

Waterfront eateries are in exactly the right place to make the most of the views, history and people-watching in this area. Sit back, sip a cold cider and enjoy.

The Cottage Inn £ ⓯ Take the ferry to its final destination along the water and stop off at this delightful pub for a drink or some traditional pub grub. ⓐ Baltic Wharf, Cumberland Road ⓣ 0117 921 5256 ⓛ 11.00–23.00 Mon–Sat, 11.00–22.30 Sun

Olive Shed £ ⓰ Mediterranean café beside the M Shed. Tapas, olives, organic wine, homemade cakes, lunch and dinner. ⓐ Princes Wharf ⓣ 0117 929 1960 ⓦ www.theoliveshed.com ⓔ info@theoliveshed.com ⓛ 10.00–22.00 Tues–Sat, 10.00–16.00 Sun, closed Mon ⓘ Booking recommended

Bordeaux Quay ££ ⓱ Bordeaux Quay is a flagship restaurant for Bristol – local, green and sustainable are the watchwords and it was lauded as the UK's first eco-restaurant when it opened in 2006, serving sophisticated European dishes. As well as a restaurant, you'll also find a deli, café, bakery and cookery school. ⓐ V-Shed, Canons Way ⓣ 0117 943 1200 ⓦ www.bordeaux-quay.co.uk ⓔ info@bordeaux-quay.co.uk

The Glassboat ££ ⑱ One of the city's most romantic venues, the Glassboat is moored at Welsh Back with views of the swans and an Italian-influenced menu. Great fish. Lunch, dinner and afternoon tea. ⓐ Welsh Back ⓣ 0117 929 0704 ⓦ www.glassboat.co.uk ⓔ restaurant@glassboat.co.uk

Mud Dock ££ ⑲ Is it a bike shop or is it a café? It's both: one upstairs and one below. Mud Dock's café has great cocktails,

🔺 Famous West Country cheeses on sale at Bordeaux Quay's delicatessen

Spanish-inspired food and a fab sun terrace overlooking the water. Great wine list, too. Better for lunch, brunch and afternoon drinks than dinner. ⓐ The Grove ⓣ 0117 929 2151 ⓦ www.mud-dock.co.uk ⓛ 10.00–17.00 Sun & Mon, 10.00–22.00 Tues–Thur, 10.00–23.00 Fri, 09.00–23.00 Sat

⬥ By night, the waterfront transforms into the centre of Bristol's nightlife

Myristica ££ ⓴ Fantastic modern Indian restaurant serving classic and reworked dishes including rabbit and squid curries as well as tikka masala. ⓐ Welsh Back ⓣ 0117 927 2277 ⓦ www.myristica.co.uk ⓛ 12.00–14.00 & 17.30–23.30 Mon–Fri, 17.30–23.30 Sat, 17.30–22.30 Sun

Riverstation ££ ㉑ Stylish modern restaurant with a dockside terrace and great views. One of Bristol's best. Downstairs is a cosy bar leading out onto the decking; upstairs the restaurant is more refined. ⓐ The Grove ⓣ 0117 914 4434 ⓦ www.riverstation.co.uk ⓛ 12.00–14.30 & 18.00–22.30 Mon–Thur, 12.00–14.30 & 18.00–23.00 Fri & Sat, 12.00–15.00 Sun

Severnshed ££ ㉒ Fine dining by the water in a former boathouse designed by Brunel. Good for cocktails; DJs on a Saturday night for an older, classy crowd. ⓐ The Grove ⓣ 0117 925 1212 ⓦ www.shedrestaurants.co.uk ⓛ 12.00–24.00 Sun–Thur, 12.00–02.00 Fri & Sat

Spyglass ££ ㉓ Great value barbecue restaurant set on a boat also serving tapas and vegetarian options where you'll find students, groups of friends and family all enjoying the alfresco-style ambience and occasional live music. ⓐ Welsh Back ⓣ 0117 927 7050 ⓦ www.spyglassbristol.co.uk

AFTER DARK

Nightlife can get rowdy around the waterfront but one thing's for sure: there's always something going on.

IN THE FOOTSTEPS OF BRUNEL

Isambard Kingdom Brunel (1806–59), with his stovepipe hat and trademark cigar, was one of the most iconic engineers of the Victorian age. His mark is all over Bristol's key visitor attractions, from the SS *Great Britain*, the first vessel of its size to cross the Atlantic, to the Clifton Suspension Bridge, and nowhere more so than the historic harbourside area. This route takes you along the Brunel Mile and the Dockside walk, both available as pamphlets from the Visitor Information Centre.

Start at Temple Meads. Brunel constructed the GWR station – not in use today – which you'll see to the right as you walk out of the station. It was completed in 1841 and was the first real railway terminus in the UK.

Cross the road beside Express by Holiday Inn and walk along Redcliffe Way. Ahead of you, you'll see St Mary Redcliffe church (see page 43). Cross the road, go over the bridge and you'll see Redcliffe Wharf and the start of the harbourside area.

Stop for coffee at Severnshed, a restaurant in a former boathouse designed by Brunel. Keep walking around the waterfront and around past the Arnolfini. Cross the bridge here and carry on along the water's edge to M Shed. Here you'll find out plenty of information about the city's seafaring history and Brunel's role in it.

Continue walking and you'll soon find yourself at the SS *Great Britain*, Brunel's iconic ship (see page 58), where an award-winning museum can fill you in on all the details about his greatest project and what it was like to travel on it. Look up to the right, across the water, and you'll see Clifton Suspension Bridge over the Avon Gorge, one of the symbols of the city.

If you choose to walk further, stop for a break at The Cottage Inn and walk around Underfall Yard, where the Bristol docks developed and Brunel worked. It's now a marina but some historical buildings remain. Catch a ferry to return to the city centre or retrace your steps back along the water, stopping at the Olive Shed for refreshments.

The Apple ❷ One of the city's top cider drinking spots, on a boat moored beside Welsh Back. The tractor fuel cocktail is particularly potent. ⓐ Welsh Back ⓣ 0117 925 3500 ⓦ www.applecider.co.uk

Oceana ❷ Bristol's biggest nightclub, with a 1980s disco room, five bars and two clubs. DJs tend towards R'n'B and disco. ⓐ South Building, Canons Road ⓣ 0845 293 2860 ⓦ www.oceanaclubs.com

Thekla ❷ One of Bristol's best clubs and live music venues; also onboard a ship, moored at Mud Dock. Hosts the Dot-to-Dot music festival in June as well as plenty of live guitar-orientated and indie music. ⓐ The Grove ⓣ 08713 100000 ⓦ www.theklabristol.co.uk ⓘ Admission charge

Clifton & the West End

The most refined area of Bristol, high on a hill overlooking the docks, Clifton offers Georgian architecture, excellent shopping, drinking and dining and some of the city's favourite green spaces. There has been talk of a lift being created to help cyclists climb Park Street but at time of writing, it is just talk.

SIGHTS & ATTRACTIONS

This area of the city offers cultural attractions, architectural gems and historical buildings as well as a wonderful country park and some great picnic spots.

Ashton Court

This country estate, just across Clifton Suspension Bridge, is a retreat enjoyed by the whole city, and is the UK's third most visited country park. The 344 ha (850 acres) of woodland and meadow are all free, and contain red and fallow deer, ancient oak trees, bluebell meadows, cycle routes, walking paths, and pitch and putt golf.

It all centres around the grand Grade II listed Ashton Court mansion, surrounded by manicured gardens which give way to fields and woodland. The estate hosts some of Bristol's biggest festivals, including the Balloon Fiesta in August, with hot-air balloon rides. ⓐ Long Ashton ⓣ 0117 963 9174 ⓦ www.ashtoncourtestate.co.uk ⓛ Daily 08.00–17.15 (Nov–Jan); 08.00–18.15 (Feb); 08.00–19.15 (Mar & Oct); 08.00–20.15 (Apr & Sept); 08.00–21.15 (May–Aug)

Brandon Hill

Tucked away behind Park Street (accessed via Great George Street, Jacob Wells Road or Berkeley Square), Brandon Hill is one of the city's oldest municipal parks, with panoramic views of the city and fantastic sunsets. Some of the area is a designated nature park, with a pond and long grass; there's also a play area, picnic spots and woodlands.

Crowning the hill is Cabot Tower, built in 1897 and offering a view of the harbourside to commemorate the 400th anniversary of John Cabot's voyage to Newfoundland. It is currently closed to the public pending restoration.

Bristol Cathedral

Bristol Cathedral, opposite the council buildings on College Green, is one of the world's finest hall churches. At the eastern end of the cathedral, the nave, choir and aisles are all the same height, making it a large hall, and singularly important in architectural terms. There has been a church here for over a thousand years. ⓐ College Green ⓣ 0117 926 4879 ⓦ www.bristol-cathedral.co.uk ⓛ 08.00 until after Evensong daily

Bristol Zoo Gardens

One of the city's top attractions, with Asiatic lions, gorillas, lemurs and penguins among the 450 species to see. There's a chance to get up close and personal with lorikeets, lemurs and butterflies, and at ZooRopia, kids can fly down zipwires and monkey about in the aerial playground. ⓐ Clifton Down ⓣ 0117 974 7300 ⓦ www.bristolzoo.org.uk ⓛ 09.00–17.30 daily ⓝ FirstGroup

buses runs a Zoo Safari Ticket including entry and bus travel
(☎ 0871 200 2233 for more information) ❶ Admission charge

Clifton Suspension Bridge
Brunel's suspension bridge has a romantic history – it started life
as a dream by a Bristol wine merchant who left a legacy in 1754 to
build a bridge over the gorge. An architectural competition was
held and 24-year-old Isambard Kingdom Brunel was given his first
major commission as the winner and project engineer. Financial
difficulties held up the build, which started in 1831, and by 1843, it
was abandoned. Brunel died without seeing his bridge completed
in 1859, but it finally opened in 1864 as his memorial. Today, the
bridge is a two-way road with pedestrian access and a small
information point, with an exhibition about its history, on the
Ashton Court side. ❸ Clifton Suspension Bridge Trust
☎ 0117 974 4664 ❺ www.clifton-suspension-bridge.org.uk
🕐 Interpretation Centre open 10.00–17.00 daily; free guided tours
of the bridge 15.00 Sun (Easter–mid-Sept)

College Green
At the foot of Park Street, between the cathedral and the city's
stunning council buildings, College Green is a popular spot
for skateboarders, teen goths and office workers picnicking
in the sun.

The Downs
Durdham Down and Clifton Down make up this 162-ha
(400-acre) green space on the edge of the city, north of Clifton.
Largely grassland, they have views of the Avon Gorge and Leigh

Woods and are popular at the weekend for sports fixtures and kite flying. Near to where the Downs meet Clifton Suspension Bridge, you'll find the Observatory, camera obscura and cave.

Georgian House

This 18th-century Georgian house is now a free museum, just off Park Street. It was built in 1790 for John Pinney, a sugar merchant and slave plantation owner, and his slave Pero, of Pero's Bridge fame, lived here with him. In the 11 rooms you can see Pinney's cold water plunge pool, formal rooms, the library and a small exhibition about the sugar trade and Pero. ⓐ 7 Great George Street ⓣ 0117 921 1362 ⓛ 10.00–17.00 Sat–Wed, closed Thur & Fri

Lido

This reinvented Victorian spa in the centre of Clifton was closed for a long time but is now the most chichi spot in the city. The café-bar serves up delicious homemade cakes, coffee and tapas while upstairs the restaurant has a Mediterranean menu. Both look out on to the pool and hot tub; spa-goers also have access to the sauna and steam room inside and spa treatments are also available. ⓐ Oakfield Place, Clifton ⓣ 0117 966 9530 (spa), 0117 933 9533 (restaurant) ⓦ www.lidobristol.com ⓔ bookings@lidobristol.com ⓘ Book in advance for spa facilities. Charge for spa, pool and facilities; café and bar free to all

The Red Lodge

You could be forgiven for thinking that Bristol's most impressive buildings are Georgian, but the Red Lodge proves you wrong. The house, dating to 1580, is a Tudor gem in the centre of the city, with Elizabethan plasterwork, carved chimneypieces and a stunning knot garden behind it. It was built as a lodge for a great house, which stood where the present Colston Hall stands today. ⓐ Park Row ① 0117 921 1360 ⓛ 10.00–17.00 Sat–Wed, closed Thur & Fri

Royal York Crescent

Bristol's answer to Bath's Royal Crescent is the Royal York Crescent in Clifton, a broad sweep of Georgian townhouses built in golden stone with terraces looking out on to the city and the docks below. They were built from 1791 to 1812 and at the time were the longest terrace in Europe; they are now private houses and flats.

University of Bristol

Bristol is one of the country's redbrick universities. Stretching over much of Clifton, it includes the Wills Memorial Building, the grand tower at the top of Park Street, and large detached houses along Woodland Road behind it. Undergraduate open days take place in June and September, and at other times of year, various events from concerts to architectural tours allow a glimpse behind the scenes. ⓐ Senate House, Tyndall Avenue ① 0117 928 9000 ⓦ www.bris.ac.uk

CULTURE

Bristol City Museum and Art Gallery

This museum at the top of Park Street tells the story of the world from the beginning of time to the present day, with a small modern art gallery, a large gallery showing stuffed animals, and regular photography and art exhibitions well worth dropping in to see. The gallery gained national acclaim in 2009 when Banksy performed a guerrilla takeover, filling the museum with his artwork. ⓐ Queen's Road ⓣ 0117 922 3571 ⓦ www.bristol.gov.uk/museums ⓛ 10.00–17.00 daily

Royal West of England Academy

This was Bristol's first art gallery. Touring exhibitions from London are well worth catching, as are the gallery tours, artist talks and demonstrations. Expect anything from local artists' rural landscapes to illustrated fairytales by David Hockney. ⓐ Queen's Road ⓣ 0117 973 5129 ⓦ www.rwa.org.uk ⓛ 10.00–17.30 Mon–Sat, 14.00–17.00 Sun ❶ Admission charge for some galleries

St George's

Tucked away off Park Street, St George's is a former church with a solid reputation for live music. The acoustics are fantastic, whether you're listening to an Estonian chamber music trio, local ensembles, jazz, blues or flamenco. ⓐ Great George Street, off Park Street ⓣ 0845 402 4001 ⓦ www.stgeorgesbristol.co.uk ⓝ Bus: 1, 8, 8A, 9, 9A

RETAIL THERAPY

This area is full of great shopping potential, with designer stores rubbing shoulders with exquisite independent boutiques. Try **Clifton Village** for presents and fashion, with **Clifton Arcade** for antiques and second-hand furniture, **Park Street** for street style, and **Whiteladies Road** for designer interiors and a small Saturday farmer's market.

Arch House Deli Opposite Clifton Arcade, this large deli sells local cheeses, salad boxes, charcuterie, wine and just about every edible goodie you can imagine and has won several food awards. ⓐ Boyce's Avenue ⓣ 0117 974 1166 ⓦ www.archhousedeli.com

Christmas Steps Linking the city centre with Park Street, Christmas Steps is a jumble of premises including small art galleries, a shoemaker, a clockmaker and a burlesque-vintage shop, as well as a chip shop at the bottom said to be one of England's oldest. The rumour persists that this street was built on top of a cemetery and that ghosts have been seen in many shops.

Diana Porter Jaw-dropping contemporary jewellery from a raft of local and UK independent designers and Diana Porter herself. ⓐ 33 Park Street ⓣ 0117 909 0225 ⓦ www.dianaporter.co.uk ⓔ web@dianaporter.co.uk

The Guild Founded in 1908, the Bristol Guild of Applied Art sells beautiful gifts and designer homewares on the ground floor, with art, crafts and furniture upstairs. If you're there around lunch time, there is also a fantastic value café on the second floor. ⓐ 68–70 Park Street ⓣ 0117 926 5548 ⓦ www.bristolguild.co.uk

TAKING A BREAK

You won't go hungry or thirsty round here, with plenty of chain and independent cafés, bars and restaurants to choose from.

Boston Tea Party £ ㉗ Independent café with a sunny garden serving soups, sandwiches and salads plus a huge range of teas and coffees and homemade cakes. ⓐ 75 Park Street ❶ 0117 929 8601 ⓦ www.bostonteaparty.co.uk

Rocotillos £ ㉘ Retro 1950s-style diner that has starred in *Skins*. Great thick ice-cream milkshakes and burgers to die for. ⓐ 1 Queen's Road ❶ 0117 929 7207

Budokan ££ ㉙ Pan-Asian flavours in an unlikely setting beside a shopping centre; don't let that put you off – this is Wagamama done very well. ⓐ 1 Whiteladies Gate ❶ 0117 949 3030

The Clifton Sausage ££ ㉚ Friendly, relaxed restaurant with pub stylings and the best sausages in town – with at least six varieties to choose from each day, plus a taster plate. ⓐ 7–9 Portland Street ❶ 0117 973 1192 ⓦ www.cliftonsausage.co.uk ❺ Restaurant and bar open daily and Bank Holiday Monday at varying times

Goldbrick House ££ ㉛ One of Bristol's best restaurants, with a café downstairs and cocktail bars upstairs, serving modern British food in refined, glamorous rooms. ⓐ 69 Park Street ❶ 0117 945 1950 ⓦ www.goldbrickhouse.co.uk

BANKSY'S BRISTOL

Banksy grew up in Bristol and the city bears so many marks from his spraycan that it draws hipster visitors every year just to see them.

In June 2009, he staged his summer show at the Bristol City Museum and Art Gallery, where he installed over 100 pieces of art, from animatronic budgies and fur coats to rude reinventions of classic paintings.

Banksy's other works can be seen outdoors around the city. Start at Park Street, where by the bridge at the bottom you can see a naked man hanging out of a window while a semi-clad woman and her husband look on. Opposite the Bristol Royal Infirmary on Upper Maudlin Street, you can see a police marksman with his sights trained across the road, with a boy standing behind him.

Graffiti mecca Stokes Croft should be your next stop. Here you'll find plenty of multicoloured murals and above a newsagents shop, Banksy's 'Mild Mild West' scene, of a teddy bear throwing a Molotov cocktail at assembled riot policemen.

Elsewhere, Easton's streets also have a huge number of tags and pictures. The key graffiti to look for includes some work on Robertson Road and a gorilla wearing a pink facemask where Sandy Lane and Stapleton Road meet.

For further information about Banksy, visit Ⓦ www.banksy.co.uk; and for a map showing all of Bristol's top street art locations: Ⓦ www.bristol-street-art.co.uk

Thali Café ££ ❷ This café serves up its renowned thalis with a range of curries and the added bonus of a Bollywood cocktail bar. A Bristol legend, the chain was crowned Radio 4's takeaway of the year in 2010 for its Mumbai-styled tiffin boxes.
ⓐ 1 Regent St ❶ 0117 974 3793 ⓦ www.thethalicafe.co.uk
🕒 10.00–24.00 Tues–Sun, 18.00–24.00 Mon

AFTER DARK

Whiteladies Road is a hub of student nightlife with blaring music and alcopops everywhere; **Park Street** has more of the same. **Clifton Village**, however, is far more refined with an upmarket atmosphere and an older vibe; **The Triangle** is somewhere between the two.

🔺 *Clifton's Regency and Georgian houses look out towards the Clifton gorge*

The Avon Gorge Hotel ㉝ This hotel is possibly the best spot in town for views of Clifton Suspension Bridge. Often full of uni students and their parents, there are barbecues on the terrace in summer and an ice rink in winter. ⓐ Sion Hill, Clifton ⓣ 0117 973 8955 ⓦ www.theavongorge.com

The Coronation Tap ㉞ Legendary Bristol cider pub in the backstreets of Clifton. Their trademark Exhibition Cider is so strong they won't serve it in a glass – you'll have to make do with plastic. ⓐ 8 Sion Place ⓣ 0117 973 9617 ⓦ www.thecoronationtap.com

Haus ㉟ At the top of Whiteladies Road bordering the Downs, this is the cocktail bar to be seen in, a snug Berlin-style speakeasy with the best drinks in town. Knock on the door for admittance. ⓐ 52 Upper Belgrave Road ⓣ 0117 946 6801 ⓦ www.hausbar.co.uk ⓛ 20.00–02.00 daily ⓘ Groups of five or more must book in advance

The Woods ㊱ Well known for its whisky-tasting nights, outdoor patio and strange insects and taxidermy on the wall. ⓐ 1 Park Street Avenue ⓣ 0117 925 0890

▶ *Relax in style at Thermae Bath Spa*

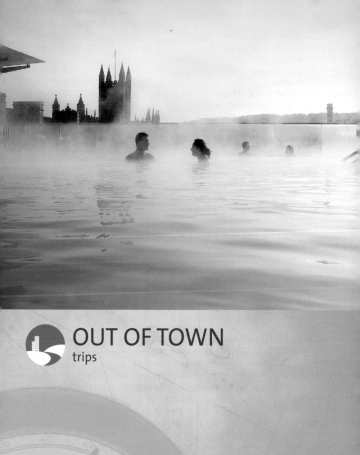

OUT OF TOWN
trips

Bath

Just 21 km (13 miles) from Bristol, the spa city of Bath is blessed with Georgian architecture, honey-coloured Bath stone buildings and plenty to do. The highlights are two watery attractions: at the **Roman Baths** you can visit the ancient ruins of the city's original spa and at the **Thermae Bath Spa** you can enjoy the water in an ultra-modern setting.

GETTING THERE

The train from Temple Meads takes 12 minutes and runs every 30 minutes (📞 08457 000 125 🌐 www.firstgreatwestern.co.uk). The X39 bus runs from Bristol's central station to Bath every 12 minutes and takes about 40 minutes (📞 0871 200 2233 🌐 www.firstgroup.com). If you are driving from central Bristol, take the A4 and park in Newbridge Park and Ride. Central Bath has parking problems and a confusing one-way system.

Bath Tourist Information Centre ⓐ Abbey Chambers, Abbey Churchyard 📞 0844 847 5256 🌐 www.visitbath.co.uk

SIGHTS & ATTRACTIONS

Bath Abbey

The abbey is Bath's most impressive building, finished in 1499 and standing on the site of two previous churches dating back to the 8th century. ⓐ 12 Kingston Buildings 📞 01225 422462 🌐 www.bathabbey.org ✉ office@bathabbey.org 🕐 09.00–16.30 Mon–Sat, 13.00–14.30 & 16.30–17.30 Sun ❶ Charge for tours

Georgian Bath

Bath's key architectural treasures are the Royal Crescent,
Pulteney Bridge and the Circus. No 1 Royal Crescent is a
restored townhouse showing life in the 18th century;
Pulteney Bridge dates to 1773 and overlooks a beautiful
horseshoe-shaped weir; and the Circus, inspired by the Roman
Coliseum, is a curved section of elegant townhouses dating to
1768. ❷ No 1 Royal Crescent ☎ 01225 428126
🌐 www.bath-preservation-trust.org.uk 🕐 Tues–Sun 10.30–17.00
(Feb–late Oct); 10.30–16.00 (end Oct–Dec), closed Mon
❶ Admission charge; Pulteney Bridge and the Circus are free

The Roman Baths

In use since the 4th century AD until the late 1970s, the Roman
Baths make use of Bath's natural spring water, which comes out
of the ground at 46°C (115°F). There's plenty to see, including

🔺 Pulteney Bridge has shops across the full span on both sides

Roman coins and Victorian sculptures. ⓐ Stall Street
🕿 01225 477785 ⓦ www.romanbaths.co.uk
ⓔ romanbaths_bookings@bathnes.gov.uk 🕒 Daily 09.30–16.30
(Jan, Feb, Nov & Dec); 09.00–17.00 (Mar–June, Sept & Oct);
09.00–21.00 (July & Aug) ❶ Admission charge

Thermae Bath Spa

Enjoy the city's natural mineral-rich waters. The main spa has
an underground pool, a rooftop pool and a floor of
aromatherapy steam rooms and foot baths; across the road
the smaller Cross Bath has a fountain bubbling up from the
earth. Book in advance. ⓐ Hot Bath Street 🕿 0844 888 0844
ⓦ www.thermaebathspa.com 🕒 09.00–22.00 daily
(last entry 17.30) ❶ Admission charge

CULTURE

Fashion Museum

Collection of fashion from the 1600s to the present day.
Visiting exhibitions are worth looking out for. ⓐ Bennett Street
🕿 01225 477173 ⓦ www.fashionmuseum.co.uk 🕒 Daily 10.30–
17.00 (Mar–Oct); 10.30–16.00 (Jan, Feb, Nov & Dec)
❶ Admission charge

The Jane Austen Centre and Regency Tea Room

Jane Austen lived in Bath from 1801 to 1806 at No 25 Gay Street
and this museum offers a slice of Regency life with costumes,
guides and exhibitions. ⓐ 40 Gay Street 🕿 01225 443000
ⓦ www.janeausten.co.uk 🕒 Daily 11.00–16.30 (Nov–Feb);

09.45–17.30 (Mar–June, Sept & Oct); 09.45–19.00 Thur–Sat (July & Aug) ❶ Admission charge

Theatre Royal

Incorporating The Egg, a theatre space for children, as well as The Ustinov, an edgier venue, the Theatre Royal dates to 1805. Touring West End productions frequent the main theatre, with pantomimes at Christmas. ⓐ Sawclose ❶ 01225 448844 Ⓦ www.theatreroyal.org.uk

Victoria Art Gallery

One of the best art galleries in the region, with a collection from the 15th century to the present day and an exciting temporary exhibition programme. ⓐ Bridge Street ❶ 01225 477233 Ⓦ www.victoriagal.org.uk 🕙 10.00–17.00 Tues–Sat, 13.30–17.00 Sun, closed Mon

RETAIL THERAPY

SouthGate Centre Bath's newest shopping centre is all about youthful fashion, upmarket stylings and desirable electronics. ⓐ 12 Southgate Street ❶ 01225 469061 Ⓦ www.southgatebath.com 🕙 09.00–18.00 Mon–Sat, 11.00–17.00 Sun

TAKING A BREAK

The Fine Cheese Co £ Relaxed café in the city's finest cheese emporium, serving lunches, snacks and afternoon tea.

🅐 29 & 31 Walcot Street 🕕 01225 448748
🅦 www.finecheese.co.uk 🕒 09.30–17.30 Mon–Fri, 09.00–17.30
Sat, closed Sun

Demuths ££ Highly regarded vegetarian restaurant serving
innovative dishes, tea, coffee and cakes. 🅐 2 North Parade
Passage 🕕 01225 446059 🅦 www.demuths.co.uk 🕒 10.00–17.00
& 17.30–22.00 Sun–Fri, 09.00–17.00 & 17.30–22.00 Sat

River Cottage Canteen ££ Hugh Fearnley-Whittingstall's local,
organic, fair trade café. 🅐 22–23 Westgate Street 🕕 01225 471578
🅦 www.rivercottage.net 🕒 Daily for breakfast, lunch and
afternoon tea, dinner Wed–Sun only 🛈 Dinner bookings
advisable

The Olive Tree £££ Acclaimed restaurant at The Queensberry
Hotel using locally sourced produce. 🅐 Russell Street
🕕 01225 447928 🅦 www.thequeensberry.co.uk

AFTER DARK

Blue Rooms Underground VIP-style club in central Bath.
🅐 George Street 🕕 01225 470040 🅦 www.bluerooms.net
🅔 info@bluerooms.net 🛈 Admission charge

Grappa Grown-up stylish bar with fantastic wine list, antipasti
and pizzas. Worth climbing the hill for. 🅐 3 Belvedere, Lansdown
🕕 01225 448890 🅦 www.grappabar.co.uk

ACCOMMODATION

Bath Central Travelodge £ No-frills hotel rooms in the city centre. ⓐ 1 York Buildings, George Street ⓣ 0871 984 6219 ⓕ 01225 442061 ⓦ www.travelodge.co.uk

The Halcyon ££ Great value city centre hotel with boutique touches. ⓐ 2–3 South Parade ⓣ 01225 444100 ⓕ 01225 331200 ⓦ www.thehalcyon.com ⓘ Breakfast not included

The Royal Crescent £££ The city's most elegant five-star hotel. ⓐ 16 Royal Crescent ⓣ 01225 823333 ⓦ www.royalcrescent.co.uk

Bristol to Bath by bike
This route follows the path of an old railway so is thankfully flat, and there are several cafés en route. At 13 miles long, it makes a nice afternoon cycle. From Bath, you can return by train with your bike.

Cumberland Basin to Pill
Starting on Cumberland Road and crossing bridges to the south side of the river, the route takes you along the bottom of the Cumberland Basin, beneath the suspension bridge, through Leigh Woods and out to the village of Pill. It's an afternoon's cycle on paths where you might see horses and walkers but not much else.

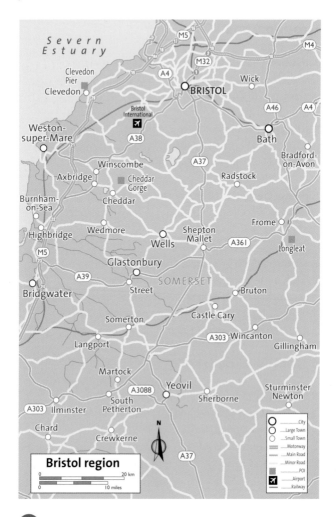

Bristol region

Severn Estuary

Clevedon Pier
Clevedon

Wick

BRISTOL

Bristol International

Weston-super-Mare

Bath

Bradford-on-Avon

Winscombe

Axbridge
Cheddar Gorge
Cheddar

Radstock

Burnham-on-Sea

Frome

Wedmore

Shepton Mallet

Longleat

Highbridge

Wells

SOMERSET

Glastonbury

Bridgwater

Street

Bruton

Somerton

Castle Cary

Langport

Wincanton

Gillingham

Martock

Yeovil

Sturminster Newton

Ilminster

South Petherton

Sherborne

Chard

Crewkerne

N

⭘	City
⭘	Large Town
○	Small Town
	Motorway
	Main Road
	Minor Road
◼	POI
✈	Airport
	Railway

0   20 km
0   10 miles

Somerset

Somerset is an overlooked county, bypassed by visitors heading to the honeypots of Devon and Cornwall, but it has plenty to offer within a short drive. Most attractions can be visited in a day trip from Bristol.

For special offers, accommodation booking and tempting tours, including cycle and cider routes, contact Visit Somerset (☎ 01934 750833 ⓦ www.visitsomerset.co.uk).

GETTING THERE

The 376 bus runs from Bristol to Glastonbury; change at Wells for the 670 to Wookey Hole and the 126 to Cheddar (1 hr 15 mins, hourly). The X1 and 353 run from Bristol to Weston-super-Mare (1 hr, twice-hourly) (☎ 0871 200 2233 ⓦ www.firstgroup.com). Trains run from Temple Meads to Weston-super-Mare (30 mins, twice-hourly) (☎ 08457 000 125 ⓦ www.firstgreatwestern.co.uk).

SIGHTS & ATTRACTIONS

Cheddar Gorge

Cheddar Gorge is a Site of Special Scientific Interest with limestone cliffs dating back 300 million years, caves, rare plants and animals. ☎ 01934 742343 ⓦ www.cheddarcaves.co.uk ⏱ Visitor centre and attractions daily 10.00–17.30 Easter, May, Whitsun school holiday, July & Aug; 10.30–17.00 rest of the year ⓝ Bus: 126, 376 ❶ Admission charge

Clevedon Pier

Clevedon was a popular Victorian seaside resort. A walk along the UK's only Grade I listed pier is not to be missed, complete with views of the Severn Estuary and an ice cream at the end. **☎** 01275 878846 **ⓦ** www.clevedonpier.com **🕐** 10.00–17.00 Mon–Fri, 10.00–18.00 Sat & Sun (late Mar–Oct); 10.00–16.00 Mon–Fri, 10.00–17.00 Sat & Sun (Nov–mid-Mar) **❶** Admission charge

Glastonbury

Known variously for its links to Arthurian myth and legend, its role in the history of Christianity and its world-famous music festival, Glastonbury has plenty going on. Climb **Glastonbury Tor** (shuttle buses available from the town centre) for a view of the Somerset Levels, visit the peaceful **Glastonbury Abbey** or wander around the town's many mystical shops. **ⓐ** Glastonbury Abbey **☎** 01458 832267 **ⓦ** www.glastonburyabbey.com **🕐** Daily 10.00–16.30 (Dec & Jan); 10.00–17.00 (Feb); 09.30–17.30 (Mar); 09.30–18.00 (Apr, May & Sept); 09.00–18.00 (June–Aug); 09.30–17.00 (Oct); 09.30–16.30 (Nov) **ⓝ** Bus: 376 **❶** Admission charge; Glastonbury Tor is free

Longleat

Technically (just) in Wiltshire, eccentric Lord Bath's mansion and safari park is a hit with families and visitors around the county. Watch out for monkeys on top of your car and grizzled tigers trying to keep pace with vehicles. **☎** 01985 844400 **ⓦ** www.longleat.co.uk **🕐** 10.00–16.00 Mon–Fri, 10.00–17.00 Sat & Sun (Mar–Oct) **❶** Admission charge

Weston-super-Mare

Whether you're a kitsch kiss-me-quick type or prefer your adventure sports, there's something for you here in under an hour's drive from Bristol, from donkey rides to buggy surfing. Fish'n'chips are a must. ⓐ Weston-super-Mare Tourist Information Centre, Beach Lawns ❶ 01934 888800 ❶ 01934 641741 ⓦ www.weston-super-mare.com ⓝ Bus: 353, X1 ❶ Weston-super-Mare's beach is muddy and the mudflats here are very dangerous to walk on at low tides

TAKING A BREAK

Sharpham Park £ Chic country café serving tasty organic, GM-free snacks, with a great butcher's and farm shop attached. ⓐ Kilver Court Gardens & Sharpham Park Shop, Kilver Street, Shepton Mallet ❶ 01749 340410 ⓦ www.sharphampark.com ⓛ 09.00–16.30 Mon–Fri, 09.30–17.00 Sat–Sun

🔺 Clevedon's Grade I listed pier has fantastic views of Wales

The Pilgrims at Lovington ££ Pub with rooms and restaurant serving the very best of Somerset's produce, delicious ice creams and cheese to die for. ⓐ Pilgrim's Way, Lovington ⓣ 01963 240600 ⓦ www.thepilgrimsatlovington.co.uk ⓛ 19.00–23.00 Tues, 12.00–14.30 & 19.00–23.00 Wed–Sat, 12.00–14.30 Sun. Open for bar snacks and drinks outside these hours

Miller's at Glencot House £££ This Victorian mansion hotel offers a theatrical fine-dining experience alongside antiques and curios collected by the founder of Miller's antiques guides. ⓐ Glencot Lane, Wookey Hole, Wells ⓣ 01749 677160 ⓦ www.glencothouse.co.uk ⓛ 24 hours

ACCOMMODATION

Lord Poulett Arms £ Acclaimed gastropub with country-boutique-style rooms. ⓐ High Street, Hinton St George ⓣ 01460 73149 ⓦ www.lordpoulettarms.com

Westbrook House £ B&B set in 1.6 ha (4 acres) of land, near to Glastonbury and good for walkers. ⓐ West Bradley, Glastonbury ⓣ 01458 850604 ⓦ www.westbrook-bed-breakfast.co.uk

The Bath Arms ££–£££ Quirky boutique hotel on the Longleat Estate. ⓐ The Longleat Estate, Horningsham, Warminster ⓣ 0844 815 0099 ⓦ www.batharms.co.uk ⓔ enquiries@batharms.co.uk

● *Temple Meads Railway Station is the gateway to travel in the southwest*

PRACTICAL
information

Directory

GETTING THERE

By air

Bristol International Airport is 13 km (8 miles) south of the city and can be reached from UK airports. ☏ 0871 334 4444 🌐 www.bristolairport.co.uk ✉ enquiries@bristolairport.com

Air Southwest flies from Leeds Bradford, Manchester, Newcastle and Newquay (☏ 0870 241 8202 🌐 www.airsouthwest.com). **easyJet** flies from Newcastle, Belfast, Inverness, Edinburgh and Glasgow (🌐 www.easyjet.com).

The **Bristol Flyer** coach leaves every 10 minutes and takes 35 minutes to reach the city centre. Return tickets are better value than two singles and it stops at Temple Meads, Clifton and Bristol Coach Station. 🌐 http://flyer.bristolairport.co.uk ✉ airportexpress@bristolairport.com

Checker Cars runs the airport's taxi service and charges around £30 to reach the centre. ☏ 01275 475000 🌐 www.checkercars.com

If you are driving, take the A38 from the airport towards Bristol. Pass Bristol City football ground, join the A4 and follow to the city centre.

Many people are aware that air travel emits CO_2, which contributes to climate change. You may be interested in the possibility of lessening the environmental impact of your flight through the charity **Climate Care** (🌐 www.jpmorganclimatecare.com), which offsets your CO_2 by funding environmental projects around the world.

By rail

Bristol has two main railway stations, Temple Meads and Parkway. Temple Meads is the more central and connected; regular trains link Parkway and Temple Meads. It takes 1hr 40 mins to reach Temple Meads from London Paddington.

First Great Western ☎ 08457 000 125
ⓦ www.firstgreatwestern.co.uk
National Rail Enquiries ☎ 08457 48 49 50
ⓦ www.nationalrail.co.uk

By road

Bristol is around 195 km (120 miles) west of London and easily reachable by motorway. Follow the M4 west and take the M32 at junction 19 into the city centre.

It is around 145 km (90 miles) south of Birmingham. Follow the M5 south to junction 15, then the M4 until junction 19, then the M32 to the centre. From the southwest, follow the M5 north to junction 19 and continue into Clifton and the centre.

GETTING AROUND

The **City Sightseeing** bus offers a 75-minute hop-on, hop-off tour of the main attractions. This works out as a good value option, comparing favourably with local buses. ☎ 0333 321 0101
ⓦ www.citysightseeingbristol.co.uk

Another leisurely way to see the sights is from the water. **The Bristol Ferry Boat Company** sails in a loop from the city centre, both to Hotwells and to Temple Meads, and back. It's a good way to get orientated. ☎ 0117 927 3416
ⓦ www.bristolferry.com ⓔ trips@bristolferry.com

HEALTH, SAFETY & CRIME

Bristol has a high standard of healthcare and there are few hazards beyond traffic and typical city problems. Remember to wear a helmet and pay attention to traffic when riding a bike.

Crime is a different matter. Bristol's car crime statistics are some of the worst in the UK. Be vigilant and apply usual precautions: lock car doors, put valuables out of sight and keep an eye on your wallet and handbag. Watch out for pickpockets at night.

Casualty/A&E ⓐ Bristol Royal Infirmary, Upper Maudlin Street ⓣ 0117 923 0000

NHS Walk-in Centre ⓐ 35 Broad Street ⓣ 0117 906 9610 ⓛ 08.00–20.00 Mon–Sat, 10.00–18.00 Sun & Bank Holidays

Bristol Dental Hospital (emergencies) ⓐ Lower Maudlin Street ⓣ 0117 928 4383 ⓛ From 08.00 Mon–Fri, closed Sat & Sun

Police, fire, ambulance (emergencies) ⓣ 999

Police (non-emergencies) ⓐ New Bridewell Police Station, Rupert Street ⓣ 0845 456 7000 ⓦ www.avonandsomerset.police.uk ⓛ 09.30–17.00 Mon–Fri, closed Sat & Sun

TOILETS

The Mall has some public toilets as well as a Parent & Baby room and toddler toilet (ⓐ 25 Union Gallery, Broadmead ⓛ 09.00–18.00 Mon–Sat, 11.00–17.00 Sun). Cabot Circus has toilets with disabled facilities and baby change facilities are next to the toilets, with nappy vending machines and baby food heating facilities (ⓐ Glass House ⓛ 10.00–20.00 Mon–Sat, 11.00–17.00 Sun). Otherwise, visit one of Bristol's many pubs, bars or cafés.

CHILDREN

As UK cities go, Bristol is pretty child-friendly with plenty
of attractions and summer festivals geared up specifically
for families. Parks, museums and walks along the river are
all good activities to try. The book *Children's Bristol*
(ⓦ www.childrensbristol.co.uk) provides many family-friendly
ideas. The following attractions also appeal to families:

At-Bristol (see page 54) Bring science to life at this museum,
which concentrates on keeping young minds active.
City farms Just outside the centre, two free farms have a small
selection of farm animals and delightful cafés and are perfect
for families (ⓐ St Werburghs City Farm, Watercress Road, St
Werburghs; Windmill Hill City Farm, Philip Street, Bedminster).
SS *Great Britain* (see page 58) Visit especially for the interactive
section, which brings Victorian seafaring to life.

TRAVELLERS WITH DISABILITIES

Most attractions in Bristol are disabled-friendly, but hills and
bumpy pavements leave a lot to be desired. The website
ⓦ www.gettingaboutgreaterbristol.org is a specialist resource,
with information on hotels, attractions and getting around. Bristol
Council's Health and Social Care department can also help with
queries (ⓣ 0117 922 2700 ⓛ 09.00–17.00 Mon–Fri, closed Sat & Sun).

FURTHER INFORMATION

Local listings magazines also provide a wealth of information.
Try *Venue*, available from most newsagents and some cafés, or
Folio, *The Cut* and *Shipshape* in cafés, bars and boutiques.

ACKNOWLEDGEMENTS

The photographs in this book were taken by Zenna West for
Thomas Cook Publishing, to whom the copyright belongs, except for
the following:
iStockphoto page 87 (David Woolfenden)

Project editor: Diane Teillol
Copy editor: Karolin Thomas
Proofreaders: David Salkeld & Michele Greenbank
Layout: Julie Crane
Indexer: Penelope Kent

ABOUT THE AUTHOR

Originally from Manchester, Laura Dixon was lured to Bristol by a
boyfriend seven years ago and now calls the city home. She's a regular
writer for the UK style and travel media and her favourite things about
Bristol are the Lido, Mayfest and seeing cars loaded up with surfboards
take to the road in the summer.

Send your thoughts to
books@thomascook.com

- Found a great bar, club, shop or must-see sight that we don't feature?
- Like to tip us off about any information that needs a little updating?
- Want to tell us what you love about this handy little guidebook and
  more importantly how we can make it even handier?

Then here's your chance to tell all! Send us ideas, discoveries and
recommendations today and then look out for your valuable input
in the next edition of this title.

Email the above address (stating the title) or write to:
pocket guides Series Editor, Thomas Cook Publishing, PO Box 227,
Coningsby Road, Peterborough PE3 8SB, UK.